The Scrovegni Chapel

GIOTTO

The Scrovegni Chapel, Padua

Bruce Cole

GEORGE BRAZILLER NEW YORK

Acknowledgments

For good advice on the text, I am thankful to Linda Baden and Jody Shiffman. James Czarnecki was kind enough to grant me his *Nihil Obstat*. At George Braziller, it was a pleasure to work with Adrienne Baxter. The diagram of the Scrovegni Chapel was designed by John Sharp with the assistance of Ryan Cole.

—Bruce Cole

Published in 1993 by George Braziller, Inc.
Texts copyright © George Braziller, Inc.
Illustrations copyright © Scala Archives, New York

For information, please address the publisher:

George Braziller, Inc.
60 Madison Avenue   New York, NY 10010

LIBRARY OF CONGRESS CATALOGING-IN-PUBLICATION DATA:

Cole, Bruce, 1938-
   Giotto: The Scrovegni Chapel, Padua / Bruce Cole
   p. cm.—(The Great Fresco Cycles of the Renaissance)
   Includes bibliographical references and glossary.
   ISBN 0-8076-1310-X
   1. Giotto, 1266?–1337 —Criticism and interpretation.   2. Jesus Christ—Art.
3. Mary, Blessed Virgin, Saint—Art.   4. Capella degli Scrovegni nell'Arena (Padua, Italy)
I. Title II. Series
ND623.G6C58   1993   93-6993
759.5—dc20   CIP

Frontispiece: Giotto, detail from the *Last Judgment* (c.1305), Scrovegni Chapel, Padua. This detail shows Enrico Scrovegni, Giotto's patron, presenting a model of the chapel to the Virgin, who is flanked by two attendants. A cleric supports the model on his right shoulder. See pl. 39 for the entire *Last Judgment*.

Book Design: Adrienne Weiss
Printed by Arti Grafiche Motta, Arese, Italy

Contents

For Thies & Marion Knauf

Fresco Painting in Renaissance Italy

At the end of the Middle Ages, Italy witnessed a revival of urban life and the flourishing of trade and banking that brought much new wealth to its cities and towns. By the thirteenth century, numerous new churches, town halls, palazzi, and many other types of structures were built to accommodate the thriving and newly affluent urban dwellers. As these buildings needed to be decorated, artists were employed to furnish altarpieces and chests, to carve tombs and tabernacles, and to cover the spacious walls of the new edifices.

Fresco was perfect for this task. The medium had a long history in Italy, where it was used by the Greeks, Etruscans, and Romans. After being only sporadically employed in the Middle Ages, fresco painting in the Renaissance took on a hitherto unparalleled significance among the major arts, an importance it did not gain anywhere else in Europe. It is no accident that many of the greatest Renaissance works of art are either individual frescoes or fresco cycles, such as the Scrovegni Chapel paintings, Leonardo's *Last Supper* in Milan, Michelangelo's program for the Vatican's Sistine Chapel, and Raphael's work in the

Vatican's Stanza della Segnatura, of which the best known part today is his *School of Athens*. Indeed thousands of frescoes decorate Italy; they were created and remain today in every major center of Renaissance painting with the exception of Venice, where the damp climate caused their swift deterioration.

Fresco painting is laborious and requires extensive training and skill (see page 19-24), but because its materials are relatively inexpensive, it was far more affordable than many other large-scale types of decoration, such as stone statuary or marble revetment. Painters learned the art of fresco as young apprentices in the workshops of established masters. These workshops furnished superb artistic educations that produced generations of highly skilled fresco painters. Most painters, in addition to their work on altarpieces and other types of painted objects, worked in fresco. Artists, from the obscure to the famous, were frequently commissioned to paint frescoes. These commissions came from both powerful individuals, including popes, princes, and wealthy merchants, and from people of lesser stations, such as members of confraternities or private families of more modest means.

Many buildings in Italy contain frescoes painted during the Renaissance. In hundreds of churches, the walls of the nave, the chapels, and the sacristy are decorated with scenes from the lives of Christ, the Virgin, and the saints. While they furnished handsome decoration, these images also helped the worshipper to understand some of the basic tenets of Christianity.

Frescoes also grace the walls of Renaissance town halls and other civic buildings. These paintings, sometimes of enormous size, exalt the city and its rulers, and often depict the triumph of their armies or glorious episodes in their history. Intended to impress the citizen, the frescoed images also demonstrated the power of the city to those who visited on business or came as ambassadors. Sometimes portraits of traitors or other notorious criminals painted on the outer walls of civic buildings served as pictorial reminders of the consequenes for those who betrayed their city. Other frescoes, also civic in nature, decorated the gates of city walls. In the countryside, frescoes were painted on large roadside tabernacles. Religious and mythological scenes decorated the interior walls of palazzi and castles, often with subjects chosen to inspire virtuous behavior in family members.

In many ways, the fresco cycle represents the quintessential Renaissance work of art. When it was the product of a seamless and successful collaboration among the master artist and the members of his workshop, the fresco proved just how well the Renaissance workshop was organized. Because fresco painting demanded a high degree of skill, it was also a test of the technical ability of the artist, a quality much appreciated by Renaissance patrons. Moreover, many of the most important stylistic developments in Renaissance art appeared in fresco paintings, often in public spaces, so that these innovations could be seen and copied by other artists; for example, some of Michelangelo's earliest drawings are copies of frescoes by Giotto. In short, frescoes transmitted idioms and ideas.

Renaissance society expected fresco painters to fashion comprehensible images and stories that would sometimes inspire, often edify and educate, and always give pleasure to the eye. In all types of Renaissance frescoes this clarity of expression, seen in both idiom and narrative, is one of the period's most distinguishing and impressive attributes. In technique, style, innovation, and influence, Renaissance frescoes embody that brilliance of thought and expression that so characterizes the period in which they were painted.

The Scrovegni Chapel

From the window of a train pulling slowly into the station, a tourist's first view of Padua is quite unremarkable: a bustling industrial scene characteristic of much of northern Italy. But as one strolls through the older parts of this prosperous city, its ample charm gradually unfolds. Many visitors, however, are hurrying from the station in search of a single destination: an unassuming red brick building located in a small, leafy park. This is the Scrovegni Chapel, which houses some of the most celebrated works in the entire history of art: the fresco cycle painted by the Florentine artist Giotto around 1305.

Padua was already ancient by the early fourteenth century when the Scrovegni Chapel was being painted. It had weathered the barbarian invasions following the collapse of the Roman Empire and remained a viable entity throughout the Middle Ages. In 1164, Padua's political independence was established by its citizens. Ruled by a series of powerful families (and an occasional tyrant), the city existed as a sovereign state until its conquest by nearby Venice in 1405. Although not a republic in the modern sense of the word, its form of communal government was representative for the age.

Often called *La Dotta*, "the Learned," Padua is the birthplace of the Roman historian Livy. It is also the home of an ancient and distinguished university. Founded in 1222, its professors and students numbered among them some of the most important figures of European learning, including Vesalius, Galileo, and William Harvey. The city also houses the tomb of St. Anthony of Padua. This tomb became a major destination for pilgrims from all over Europe immediately after the saint's death in 1231. A follower of St. Francis of Assisi, St. Anthony was a famous worker of miracles, and to this day his tomb remains a source of hope for the afflicted who file daily through the immense Basilica of Sant'Antonio (called *Il Santo* by the Paduans) begun one year after the saint's death. Here the ill and the infirm still touch and kiss the tomb, praying for the curative miracles for which St. Anthony is so revered.

A long street leads from the Piazza del Santo in front of the basilica to the Scrovegni Chapel—sometimes called the Arena Chapel because of its location on the site of a Roman amphitheater. This chapel, probably completed by 1303, was built by Enrico Scrovegni, one of Padua's best known and wealthiest citizens. Enrico's father, Riginaldo (died 1289), had also been a prominent, if notorious, figure. Like some of his wealthy Paduan contemporaries, he had amassed a fortune by lending money at usurious rates, a practice that the church, and many of Riginaldo's fellow citizens, condemned as sinful. In his *Divine Comedy* (begun 1307), Dante, who was in Padua in the early fourteenth century, banished Riginaldo to the seventh circle of Hell, that region reserved for sinful usurers. Seated on burning sand and beset by fiery rain, Riginaldo, who is recognizable by the Scrovegni coat of arms on the money bag that weighs around his neck, writhes in agony as he cries out to Dante.[1] The poet's view of Riginaldo reflects the disagreeable reputation that the Scrovegni family had already gained by its rampant, but very profitable, usury.

Riginaldo's son Enrico was probably a usurer as well. Wealthy and powerful, he also seems to have been viewed with disfavor—at least one of his contemporaries called him a hypocrite and a trickster. He also suffered from the sin of pride, as evidenced by his large portrait prominently displayed in the splendid chapel that he built next to his sizable home [see opposite title page]. This "family" chapel immediately incited the anger and envy of the monks of the neighboring Eremitani Church, who, in a legal document of 1305, first complained about its bell tower with "its huge new bells," which particularly disturbed them. Then, even more bitterly, they criticized the dimensions of Enrico's building. They asked:

> *That Lord Enrico will be allowed to construct in the Arena, or in that place which is called the Arena, without prejudice to the right of others, a small church, almost in the manner of an oratory, for himself, his wife, his mother and his family, [but] that [other] people ought not to be allowed to frequent this church. He should not have built a large church there and the many other things which have been made there more for pomp, vainglory and wealth than for praise, glory and honor of God.[2]*

What the monks wanted, it seems, was the destruction, or at least the scaling back, of the building to make it into something much more modest and befitting a place for family worship, a chapel instead of a church. The monks of the Eremitani were clearly worried about competition from Enrico's new building, and their objections were probably well founded, considering the size of the chapel's residential clerical staff, which consisted of three priests and a provost.

Vainglorious or not, the Scrovegni Chapel became one of Padua's most important buildings, although Enrico was able to enjoy it for only a limited time. During the siege of 1320, he deserted his native city and fled to Venice, where he lived until his death in 1336. His remains were brought back to Padua as he had requested and placed in his tomb in the chapel.

It is evident from the monks' complaint that people were immediately flocking to the chapel, which was dedicated both to the Virgin of the Annunciation and to the Virgin of Charity.[3] Part of the reason for this popularity was the Papal Bull of 1304 issued by Enrico's friend Pope Benedict XI granting indulgences to the visitor:

> *[T]hose who, having confessed and being fully penitent, shall solemnly visit the aforementioned church [the Scrovegni Chapel] on the feasts of the Nativity, of the Purification, and of the Assumption of the Virgin, to be granted a dispensation of one year and forty days, and for those who shall solemnly visit the church for one week immediately following the feast days, we mercifully give dispensation of one hundred days from the injunction of penance.[4]*

Fig. 1. Giotto, *Crucifix* (c. 1295), Santa Maria Novella, Florence

But the chapel was also attracting visitors who came not because of the indulgences promised by the papal bull, but rather to see the frescoes by Giotto, which were either well underway or even finished by the time the monks complained in 1305. Giotto di Bondone (1266?–1337) was born in Colle di Vespignano, a remote hamlet in the mountainous Mugello region some twenty miles northwest of Florence.

Giorgio Vasari (1512–74), painter and author of the extremely valuable series of artists' biographies entitled *The Lives of the Most Famous Painters, Sculptors, and Architects,* claims that Giotto's talent was first discovered by the Florentine painter Giovanni Cimabue (c. 1240–1302?), who saw him drawing a picture of a sheep on a rock near Colle di Vespignano. Recognizing his great talent, Cimabue, so Vasari claims, brought the young Giotto to Florence to instruct him in painting.

Although there is absolutely no reason to believe that this is anything other than a pious fable, it does seem likely, on the basis of the resemblance of his work to that of Cimabue and other Florentines, that Giotto did receive his artistic training in Florence, where he began working as an independent artist probably around 1290. The first documentary evidence of Giotto in Florence dates to 1301, when he is listed as owning a house in the Santa Maria Novella quarter of the city. His early Florentine works, such as the large *Crucifix* in the Church of Santa Maria Novella [fig. 1] and the *Ognissanti Madonna* altarpiece [fig. 2] are revolutionary in nature. Giotto's artistic forerunners, such as his putative teacher, Cimabue, were the inheritors of a stylistic and interpretive tradition first established in the late Middle Ages. In Cimabue's highly symbolic *Crucifix* (c. 1285) painted for the Florentine Church of Santa Croce, the overall shape of the body, the summary treatment of the anatomy, and the rendering of the loincloth are pictographic—the form is symbolic rather than realistic [fig. 3]. Christ is not to be seen as a mortal, but instead as a god, a powerful, awesome symbol of divinity.

Cimabue's commanding *Crucifix* is the creation of a masterful artist working in a highly sophisticated style. The long, swinging lines of the monumental body curving far out across the surface of the cross; the taunt, schematic musculature of the torso; the contorted, pain-filled facial features; and the streaming, serpent-like hair that seems to have a

Fig. 2. Giotto, *Ognissanti Madonna* (c. 1305), Uffizi Gallery, Florence

15

Fig. 3. Cimabue, *Crucifix* (c. 1285), Museo dell'Opera di Santa Croce, Florence. Cimbue's *Crucifix* was badly damaged in the Florentine flood of 1966 and now exists only in fragmentary form.

life of its own all combine to form a striking symbolic image of Christ's sacrificial death.

Some twenty years later (around 1305), as part of his commission for Enrico Scrovegni's chapel, Giotto painted the story of the Crucifixion. Here one sees a crucified Christ who differs radically, both in form and content, from Cimabue's Christ [fig. 4]. The most fundamental difference arises from Giotto's understanding of Christ's nature. Unlike the epic majesty of Cimabue's painting, this Christ is a vulnerable, frail human whose image invokes sympathy rather than awe. Giotto has accomplished this by abolishing most of the old, traditional pictorial conventions in favor of a new, more effective formal construction of the human body. The patterns and highly stylized lines of Cimabue's *Crucifix* have been replaced by forms that now seem to approach our notion of depicting reality. The arms painfully pulled down by the weighty body, the sagging head with its unidealized face and matted hair, and the twisted legs of Giotto's Christ, all evoke the agony of sacrifice.

In the Scrovegni Chapel *Crucifixion*, and in the *Ognissanti Madonna*, probably painted around the same time, Giotto has rethought the images of Christ and His mother. He has made them more human and more accessible than any previous artist. They now seem to be in and of the earth, beings with a heightened presence and gravity. Such innovation is remarkable when one considers that the artists of Giotto's time were taught in a workshop system in which they were required to imitate the works of the master who supervised every aspect of their artistic education; innovation and originality were not encouraged. Moreover, most of the stories painted by Giotto in the Scrovegni Chapel, and elsewhere, had ancient, codified interpretations sanctioned by the church; his innovations in these revered subjects, when this is considered, are astounding.

Such works by Giotto as his Santa Maria Novella *Crucifix* and his *Madonna and Child with Angels* in San Giorgio alla Costa, Florence, led to early fame, and then to the commission for his most extensive and most important work: the frescoes of the Scrovegni Chapel. How and when Enrico Scrovegni first heard of the artist is unknown, but there can be little doubt that he had well-defined ideas about whom he wished to decorate his chapel. Normally, local artists were engaged for such tasks, but Enrico made a special effort to employ foreigners: not only did he bring Giotto from Florence, he also hired Giovanni Pisano (1245–1320), one of

Fig. 4. Giotto, detail, *The Crucifixion* (c. 1305), Scrovegni Chapel, Padua (see pl. 34)

Fig. 5. Giovanni Pisano, *Madonna and Child with Two Angels* (c.1305), Scrovegni Chapel, Padua. Placed in front of the tomb of Enrico Scrovegni (by Andreolo de' Santi), these statues were carved around 1305. The two angels, which are of lower quality than the Madonna and Child, may be the work of Giovanni's assistants. The Scrovegni coat of arms with the sow, which Dante identified on Riginaldo's money bag, is seen behind the recumbent figure of Enrico Scrovegni.

the most renowned Tuscan sculptors of the time, to carve the statues for his tomb [fig. 5]. The Scrovegni Chapel, for which no expense was spared, was to be a glorious monument to Enrico, to his family, and, of course, to God.

The exact chronology of the decoration of the Scrovegni Chapel cannot be established with precision. We know that Enrico bought the land for the chapel in 1300. By March 1302, he had obtained permission from the bishop of Padua to build a family chapel, and according to a now-lost inscription, the structure was dedicated on March 25, 1303, the Feast of the Annunciation. In 1304 the pope issued his grant of indulgences for visitors, and there is a reference to a consecration, perhaps of one of the chapel's several altars, in 1305. This continued record of activity suggests that by 1305 the chapel was built and ready for visitors. Unfortunately, none of the documents mentions Giotto's name. It appears reasonable, nonetheless, to assume that he must have been at work by 1305, but precisely when he began and finished the job remains a mystery.

In any case, one of the earliest decisions Enrico must have made was to have the chapel's walls completely covered with frescoes. Perhaps this is one of the reasons he sought out Giotto, who, as someone trained in Florence, a city with a tradition of fresco painting, probably had much more experience with the medium than the artists of Padua, where such painting was then uncommon. In fact, the Scrovegni Chapel paintings, which were to become an important model for many subsequent painted interiors, constitute one of the earliest major fresco cycles of northern Italy.

When Giotto first entered the chapel, its walls were completely bare. As he considered its luminous interior space (length: 20.80 m; width: 8.40 m; height: 12.80 m), lit by five tall lancet windows set into the right (southern) side of the building, he must have been delighted, for here, unmarred by any moldings or niches, was a large flat expanse perfectly suited to decorate with fresco.

The word "decorate" is here used in a specific sense, for while most frescoes are narrative in nature—that is, they use pictures to tell stories—this is not their sole, nor even their primary purpose. Instead, their considerable areas of color, shape, and line are meant both to emphasize the large areas of wall common to buildings in the Italian peninsula, and to impart a harmonious, overall decoration to the interior space they cover. In a well-wrought fresco cycle (a series of paintings, all usually narrating various parts of one or more stories), the individual paintings are all subordinated to the overall decorative scheme.

The medium of fresco is ideally suited for the painting of cycles meant to decorate large areas of wall. In essence, fresco painting is the application of pigment by brush to wet plaster spread on a wall. Once the plaster dries the paint brushed onto the wall's surface bonds to it by means of a chemical reaction. The resulting surface is durable and, if properly protected from the elements, extremely long-lasting. Although it was a difficult and demanding medium, fresco was a cheap form of decoration for large areas of wall because it used simple, inexpensive materials.

Giotto and his contemporaries were proficient in the many skills and techniques that fresco painting required, including that of master plasterer. The fresco painter would begin by laying down a coat of rough plaster, called the *arriccio*, both to smooth out the wall to be painted (which was usually made of brick or stone) and to provide a moisture barrier between the wall and the final painting. When the

Fig. 6. Masolino, detail, *Saint* (1424), Sant'Agostino, Empoli. Part of an extensive fresco cycle of the story of the True Cross, Masolino's sinopia has been revealed by the removal of the *intonaco*. The rough, grainy nature of the *arriccio* and the defining lines of Masolino's skillful sinopia drawing are here readily apparent.

plaster had dried, the painter rolled strings in charcoal or wet paint and snapped them against the wall, making vertical and horizontal guidelines. These would help him find the exact center of the area to be painted, so that he could then center the composition and correctly align the forms he was about to paint.

Next, with a charcoal stick he would work up a full-scale preparatory drawing of his subject on the plaster (after about 1450, this practice would be replaced by the use of paper cartoons, stencil-like drawings that allowed the artist to make the preparatory drawings in his studio). The charcoal drawing on the plaster would be corrected and adjusted until the artist, and often his patron, were satisfied. Then, with a brush dipped in water and sinopia (a red iron oxide pigment named after its source near Sinope in Asia Minor), the artist retraced the preparatory charcoal drawing [fig. 6]. When this sinopia drawing was dry, the underlying charcoal, which might possibly stain the final painting, was brushed off with a bunch of feathers. Now the artist was able to begin the actual painting of the fresco.

This painting was done on a second coat of finer plaster called the *intonaco*, which was troweled over the *arriccio*. Because the pigment (which was mixed with water) would bond only with plaster that was still wet, it was necessary to replaster an area only as large as the painter could paint before it dried. To do this, the second coat of plaster was applied in patches, sometimes called *giornate*, an Italian term meaning "tasks done daily," and not necessarily, as is sometimes stated, "one day's work." The painter would start putting in his patches at the top and work downward so that any drips would fall on the *arriccio* that was being covered and not on the new plaster. During this process, the sinopia draw-ing, which would gradually be covered, acted as an indispensable guide to proportion, scale, and subject for what was being painted on the patches [fig. 7]. Without the sinopia drawing, the artist would have had to invent and proportion the scene as he painted it on the second coat of plaster, a difficult, if not impossible task.

The painting of the second coat of plaster presented many difficult technical problems. For instance, the degree of wetness or dryness of the plaster when the pigment was applied could ulti-mately affect the value (the darkness or lightness), and sometimes the color, of that pigment after the plaster had dried. To keep color consistent through-out the fresco, the pigment had to be applied during the brief amount of time when the plaster was just right for painting. Thus, it was necessary for the artist to understand how plaster dried under all sorts of atmospheric conditions and to be able to paint rapidly enough to cover the whole patch while it was in the optimal condition to receive the pigments. If the plaster dried too fast or too slowly and the colors changed drastically from patch to patch, it was nec-essary to chip out the plaster and begin again, a

Fig. 7. Central Italian painter, detail, *Red Silvia Buried Alive* (c. 1430), Palazzo Trinci, Foligno. Much of the *intonaco* has fallen off the wall, revealing the underlying sinopia drawing and its relation with the fresco painting on the *intonaco* above.

laborious process indeed. Fresco is a very unforgiving medium: once the pigment is brushed into the wet plaster it is absorbed immediately and cannot be erased or easily altered.

Fresco painting is always a race against time, a race to finish painting before the plaster dries. One can imagine the need for careful planning and organization as the painter and his apprentices, surrounded by buckets of water and pots of pigment, stood on scaffolds high above the floor, feverishly applying paint to the rapidly drying surface. This process of fresco painting conditioned the way artists conceived their work. To achieve the necessary speed, the design of most frescoes, especially the earlier ones done with sinopia drawings, is ample and bold in conception and shorn of much time-consuming detail. Crisp detail is, in any case, hard to achieve in the wet, blurring pigment and absorbent plaster of fresco; the detail that is found on most frescoes is often applied with pigments mixed with egg yolks or glue after the plaster has dried.

Giotto could not have painted the Scrovegni Chapel alone—the number of frescoes and the complexity of the medium made this impossible. To help him, he must have employed assistants, probably young apprentices from his own workshop. Giotto conceived every fresco and drew the sinopia drawings on the wall, but the assistants must have had a share in the painting on the *intonaco*. Because young artists of the Renaissance were taught to imitate their master's style faithfully, large-scale collaborative works such as the Scrovegni frescoes are remarkably uniform in style. Only occasionally, such as in *The Birth of the Virgin*, can one see a figure or two whose inferior drawing reveals the hand of someone other than Giotto [pl. 7].

By studying *The Visitation* in the Scrovegni Chapel, we can see how a fresco by Giotto evolved [pl. 15]. If frescoes are examined in raking light, it is usually possible to see their system of patches. In *The Visitation* there are six patches, each outlined in white in this photograph [fig. 8]. Patch no. 1, which starts at the top of the fresco, is the largest, encompassing the small porch, the sky, and the heads of the two women to the left. Because it was mainly architecture and sky, this area could be painted rather rapidly and, hence, the patch is large. Azurite, usually used for the blue, was not fully soluble in water and therefore had to be mixed with glue and applied after the *intonaco* had dried. Because

Fig. 8.   Giotto, *The Visitation* (c. 1305), Scrovegni Chapel, Padua. The illustration shows the layout of the plaster patches on the fresco.

there was no chemical bond between the pigment and the dry plaster, the blue was unstable and often flaked off the wall, as one sees in the sky and in the robes of the attendant at the right of *The Visitation*, and in many other frescoes in the Scrovegni Chapel.

Patch no. 2 of *The Visitation* is much smaller than patch no. 1. This reduction in size was necessary because painting the figures' robes was more complicated, and thus more time-consuming, than covering the large areas of sky and architecture in the first patch. Giotto was very mindful in patch no. 2, and in all the others, to make sure that robes stayed within the boundaries of each patch. In this way, each color could be contained within its own patch, thereby avoiding the difficult task of matching colors on two different patches. Patch no. 4 includes the figure of the Virgin and the head, neck, and collar of Elizabeth, but not the rest of her body, which is in patch no. 6. The smallest patch, no. 3, was used only for the head of the Virgin, the most important area of *The Visitation* and the one that had to painted with the utmost care. The patch system of the Scrovegni Chapel is masterfully planned; from the outset, Giotto's design of each fresco must have always been informed by the technical and material necessities of fresco painting. If he had painted the same subjects in another medium with very different properties—for example, tempera paint—they would have looked substantially different; with tempera, he would have achieved a much smoother, brighter, and more detailed surface.

When one enters the Scrovegni Chapel, the effect is overwhelming and uplifting: the initial impression is of a space entirely filled with light, color, and form. A sense of restful well-being seems to fill the room. The spectator has stepped into a harmonious, balanced work of art where no area calls attention to itself; the eye wanders happily and unimpeded across the chapel's walls. This experience results from Giotto's astute understanding of fresco as decoration and as a type of painting whose first function is to cover space evenly with harmonious shape and color.

Only after one has absorbed the decorative ensemble of the chapel do thoughts arise about the nature and subject of its individual frescoes. Each of the frescoes forms part of the story of the redemption of mankind through Christ. This theme is entirely appropriate for a building that served not only as a place of worship, but also as the burial place for the Scrovegni. In order to tell this complex story as clearly as possible, Giotto subdivided the painting in the chapel into five major areas, each interrelated sequentially [fig. 9]: 1. the barrel vault covered with a star-dotted blue field on which are painted rondels containing half-length figures; 2. the side walls covered by three registers of frescoes, each separated by painted borders; 3. a fictive marble lower level containing figures of virtues and vices set into painted niches; 4. the chancel arch painted with episodes of *The Annunciation, The Visitation,* and *The Pact of Judas*; and 5. the entrance wall on which is painted a large *Last Judgment* [see p. 39].

After stepping though the chapel's door, the visitor sees the chancel arch straight ahead. At the top of this arch, God the Father dispatches Gabriel to announce the coming of Christ to the Virgin. *The Annunciation* is seen below in two frescoes painted on either side of the arch: on the left Gabriel announces the coming of Christ; on the right, across the arch, the Virgin receives his tidings [pls. 13a, 13b]. The size and prominent position of the events of the *Annunciation* reflect the chapel's dedication to this sacred incarnation, which marks the beginning of humanity's redemption.

Across the chapel from *The Annunciation* is the huge *Last Judgment* covering the entire entrance wall. *The Last Judgment*, the end of time when the human race will be judged and then either damned or blessed by Christ, closes the cycle of redemption begun in *The Annunciation* on the chancel arch. *The Last Judgment*, with its dual messages of hope and fear, was the last painting the worshipper saw upon leaving the chapel. On the left side of the base of the Cross in *The Last Judgment*, in a very conspicuous place directly above the door through which one passes to exit, is the portrait of Enrico Scrovegni [see opposite title page]. Prominently lodged in Paradise, he presents a model of his chapel, held by one of his clerics, to the Virgin and her two saintly attendants. Mary here is clearly the Virgin of the Annunciation, for she is clothed in the same robes seen in *The Annunciation* directly across the chapel.

Between *The Last Judgment* and *The Annunciation*, three bands of frescoes on the side walls and four frescoes on the chancel arch tell the story of the Virgin's parents; of the life of the Virgin; of the infancy and miracles of Christ Himself; and of

Fig. 9. View facing the chancel arch of the Scrovegni Chapel

Fig. 10. Painting program, the Scrovegni Chapel

1. The Expulsion of Joachim from the Temple
2. Joachim among the Shepherds
3. The Annunciation to St. Anne
4. Joachim's Sacrifice
5. The Dream of Joachim
6. The Meeting at the Golden Gate
7. The Birth of the Virgin
8. The Presentation of the Virgin
9. The Virgin's Suitors Presenting Their Rods
10. The Suitors' Prayer before the Rods
11. The Marriage of the Virgin
12. The Virgin's Wedding Procession
13. God the Father Dispatching Gabriel
14a.,14b. The Annunciation
         (The Angel Gabriel, The Virgin)
15. The Visitation
16. The Nativity
17. The Adoration of the Magi
18. The Presentation of Christ
19. The Flight into Egypt
20. The Massacre of the Innocents
21. Christ among the Doctors
22. The Baptism of Christ
23. The Wedding at Cana
24. The Raising of Lazarus
25. The Entry into Jerusalem
26. The Cleansing of the Temple
27. The Pact of Judas
28. The Last Supper
29. The Washing of the Feet
30. The Betrayal of Christ
31. Christ before Caiaphas
32. The Mocking of Christ
33. The Road to Calvary
34. The Crucifixion
35. The Lamentation
36. Noli Me Tangere
37. The Ascension
38. The Pentecost
39. The Last Judgment (see p. 39)
40a., 40b. Fortitude and Inconstancy

26

His Passion, Crucifixion, Resurrection, and Ascension. The narrative begun with *The Expulsion of Joachim from the Temple* ends in the scene of *The Pentecost*. The Second Coming of Christ at *The Last Judgment* will eventually complete the succession of divine events set in motion by *The Annunciation*.

Giotto arranged all the stories of the Scrovegni Chapel in a simple, easily understandable sequence [fig. 10]. The account of mankind's salvation begins in the topmost register of the right wall with the fresco of *The Expulsion of Joachim from the Temple* [pl. 1]. This episode from the life of Joachim, the Virgin's father, is, like the Annunciation, a decisive event in the Christian narrative, for it initiates the chain of events that will lead to Christ's birth.

After *The Expulsion of Joachim*, the story moves rightward through the frescoes of the upper register, stopping at the entrance wall. The narrative then continues across the chapel on the upper register of the left wall, where it again moves from left to right and then through the two frescoes of *The Annunciation* on the chancel arch. It then resumes in *The Visitation* just below the Virgin of *The Annunciation* before continuing left to right along the middle register of the right wall, right up to the entrance wall. It then proceeds left to right across the middle register of the left wall, across to *The Pact of Judas* on the left side of the chancel arch. The story then recommences in the lower right register where it makes one more rotation ending just to the left of the chancel arch in *The Pentecost*: the Descent of the Holy Ghost and the imparting of the gift of different languages to the apostles, a miracle that symbolizes the establishment of the Christian Church [pl. 38]. To understand this entire sequence of events one must turn in space to follow the course of the downward spiral of episodes from wall to wall. Viewing the path of the narrative of the Scrovegni Chapel demands, unlike most other works of art, active physical participation.

It seems improbable that a layman like Giotto would have been allowed to pick each of the many scenes that tell the story from *The Expulsion of Joachim* to *The Pentecost*. Instead, the subjects were probably chosen by a priest, maybe one of those appointed to the Scrovegni Chapel, or by a theologian, perhaps someone associated with the University of Padua. It is not always possible to trace the scriptural origin of each story, but it seems certain that at least three sources were utilized. The legends of the Virgin and her parents come mainly from the Apocryphal Gospel of St. James the Less and the Gospel of the Pseudo-Matthew. The stories for the rest of the frescoes were taken from the Gospels of the New Testament and from the nearly contemporary *Meditations on the Life of Christ*, compiled by a Franciscan friar known as the Pseudo-Bonaventura—artists frequently took a variety of biblical texts as sources for their narratives. Dating from the end of the thirteenth century, the *Meditations* is a lively compilation of stories about Christ's life. Filled with much color and anecdotal detail, it is written with admirable clarity and directness. The *Meditations* always stresses the vulnerability and humanity of Christ and the other holy protagonists. The reader is asked to participate in the holy events as though present. This often homey, poignant, and highly entertaining work found a large audience, especially among those who were unable to grasp the more obscure messages of other religious writings. It, more than the Bible, must have made Giotto's contemporaries feel close to Christ; it stresses the mortal part of His nature and depicts Him as a human being who once lived in the world and who was not entirely unlike ourselves. The

Meditations must have appealed especially to Giotto, whose approach to religious subject matter was always supremely humane and direct.

While planning the frescoes for the Scrovegni Chapel, Giotto had much to keep in mind. He had to think about the exacting technical aspects of the medium; about the overall decorative and narrative demands of the fresco cycle; and about the actual design and interpretation of each story itself. Every painting in the chapel is, in its own way, a masterful solution to all these often competing necessities.

These solutions are readily apparent in *The Expulsion of Joachim from the Temple*, which begins the Scrovegni cycle. Giotto knew that the fictive space here, and in every fresco, had to be rigidly controlled. No areas of deep spatial recession could be painted, because they would create window-like holes that would visually puncture the flat surface of the walls. For Giotto and his contemporaries, fresco painting was meant to enhance and decorate the wall, not to deny it. Consequently, in *The Expulsion of Joachim* and in all the other frescoes, there is only a minimal indication of spatial depth. The temple is placed on a narrow strip of ground that ends decisively at the flat, blue sky; space develops across the surface of the fresco rather than into it. Moreover, each object and figure moves laterally across the surface of the wall, rather than backward into space.

No color, either in *The Expulsion of Joachim* or elsewhere in the chapel, is allowed to predominate and thus disturb the harmony of color that evenly covers, decorates, and emphasizes the surface of the walls. The bright but limited range of colors—deep red, creamy white, light green, and pink—are seen in many of the other frescoes in the chapel. A fixed number of handsome colors—white, red, blue, green, mauve, pink, violet, and yellow-gold—link all the frescoes together by their measured and frequent repetition. Color also aids in the narrative by clearly delineating objects and figures.

Giotto intelligently exploited the limitations imposed on him by the technical, decorative, and narrative demands of the Scrovegni Chapel frescoes. For example, in *The Expulsion of Joachim,* the need to limit spatial recession allowed him to concentrate all the action in the foreground; such compression both heightens the drama and places it close to the onlooker. The broadness, fluidity, and boldness with which each object is painted are the perfect expression of the sureness and speed required for successful fresco painting. And, because the entire narrative scheme was planned on the site at one time, *The Expulsion of Joachim* and every other fresco in the chapel constitute a formal and iconographic ensemble remarkable for its seamless unity.

All the frescoes are unified by Giotto's interpretation of narrative. In each story, he depicts the absolute peak of psychic and physical drama. More than any artist before him, he portrays this drama primarily through the depiction of intense human emotions. He does away with all superficial elements of the story; he is a minimalist whose works are reductive rather than additive. And his main focus is always on the men and women who form the hub of the drama.

The Expulsion of Joachim serves as a good introduction to the essence of Giotto's interpretive genius [fig. 11]. The temple, like a stage set, is represented only by its outer walls; there is nothing cluttering or anecdotal here. Inside these walls are the tabernacle and pulpit, the symbols of the temple's two major functions of worship and preaching. Just four figures appear: the pathetic old Joachim, whose sacrifice has been rejected because his barrenness is a sign of God's disfavor; the two priests; and

Fig. 11. Giotto, *The Expulsion of Joachim from the Temple* (c. 1305), Scrovegni Chapel, Padua (see pl. 1)

a young man kneeling inside the temple's walls. Giotto has made the temple the armature around which the action is wrapped; here and throughout the Scrovegni Chapel, architecture and landscape effectively organize and articulate the drama. The colors of *The Expulsion of Joachim* also aid in the explication of drama by decisively demarcating objects and figures.

Throughout the Scrovegni Chapel frescoes, Giotto explores the profoundest emotions. In *The Expulsion of Joachim,* for example, the action centers around acceptance and rejection. The rejected Joachim, still clutching his unwanted sacrificial sheep, is literally thrown out of the temple, while inside its sacred precincts a young father receives a priest's blessing. The physical and spatial opposition of the old Joachim about to be pushed off the temple's step with the man inside forms a perfect illustration of the conflicting emotional poles of the story. Every element in the fresco is centered around this defining moment that begins the story of the Virgin's parents.

Two of the four figures in *The Expulsion of Joachim* face rightward, and the arm and massive hanging sleeve of the priest pushing Joachim also move in that direction. Joachim moves toward the right, but he turns back longingly toward the temple at the left. In this fresco, and throughout the Scrovegni Chapel narratives, there is a steady left-right movement of figures that helps to maintain the unceasing left-to-right movement of the narratives across the chapel's walls. Occasionally, as in the turn of Joachim's head, there are significant exceptions to this, but they always make a narrative point.

In his frescoes, Giotto often uses the most elemental aspects of painting—color, line, shape, and space—as visual metaphors. At the far right of *The Expulsion of Joachim* there is a considerable amount of empty space—in the nineteenth century one historian even wondered if that space had originally been filled with something. But the area's emptiness is quite deliberate! The far right of every fresco in the Scrovegni Chapel is a place of considerable importance because it is the threshold to the next fresco in the series. Here Joachim is being pushed off into a void symbolic both of God's disfavor and of his own expulsion from God's earthly temple. The abyss at the far right eloquently expresses these concepts. Only an artist of Giotto's talent would have dared to begin on such an inauspicious note.

In the next five frescoes, God's favor shines on Joachim and his wife, Anne, who both learn through angelic visitations that they will at long last have a child: the Virgin Mary. The culminating moment of this first register, begun by *The Expulsion of Joachim*, occurs in the register's last fresco, *The Meeting at the Golden Gate*, where Joachim and Anne meet for the first time since Joachim's sacrifice, each now knowing that they will have a child. The Franciscans believed that the Virgin was conceived when they kissed, so this first moment of her life was also the first act of mankind's redemption by God [fig. 12; see also pl. 6].

Both *The Expulsion of Joachim* and *The Meeting at the Golden Gate* are, like every other fresco in the Scrovegni Chapel, fully independent compositions, self-sufficient units with individual stories told in a complete and masterful way. But because Giotto conceived of the chapel as an integrated whole, he carefully linked the frescoes with a subtle network of formal and narrative connections. Consequently, when considered together, *The Expulsion of Joachim* and *The Meeting at the Golden Gate* are considerably more complex and meaningful than when they are seen alone.

In *The Meeting at the Golden Gate*, the gate both closes the right side of the register by its massive, rooted bulk and creates the feeling of stability and calm that is the heart of the story. By contrast, the open, spiky temple with its sharp corners in *The Explusion of Joachim* is tipped up and unstable, as though it were about to slip off the narrow strip of ground. The dissimilarity among the stage-set architecture of all of the frescoes heightens and enriches the emotional difference of each drama. The actions and forms of the figures are also distinct and appropriate to their respective contexts. In *The Expulsion of Joachim*, Joachim struggles with the priest at the edge of the void into which he is about to fall, his anguish mirrored in his face and in the contortion of his body. These struggling forms contrast sharply with the stable arch-like shape formed by the unified bodies of the embracing Joachim and Anne in *The Meeting at the Golden Gate*. This human arch is amplified and echoed by a series of other arches in the fresco: the two haloes, the arch of the Golden Gate, and the arches of the bridge. These shapes create an interwoven harmony that mirrors the joy of the old couple as the narrative sequence of the first register is brought to a close. Throughout the Scrovegni frescoes there are many other such enriching contrasts among the paintings.

Because documentary evidence on Giotto's life is scarce, we have only partial knowledge of what he did after the Scrovegni Chapel. By 1313, Giotto had been in Rome, for in that year he employed an agent to recover certain household goods that he had left there, perhaps while working on the now badly damaged mosaic in the portico of St. Peter's. A document of 1318 reveals that by that time he already had a son and a daughter; he was to father eight children in all. Other records from throughout his working life demonstrate that he made money from several nonartistic ventures, such as renting out looms and leasing and purchasing farmland. A series of documents from 1328 to 1334 reveals Giotto's presence in Naples, where he worked for King Robert, who styled the artist *familiaris et fidelis noster* (our faithful friend) and gave him a pension. During the decade from 1325 to 1335, Giotto also worked in the Franciscan church of Santa Croce in Florence. Here, in the Bardi and Peruzzi chapels, he painted two fresco cycles that remain his most extensive extant work in the city. Contemporary evidence suggests that he did other frescoes in Florence, but these, along with many altarpieces, unfortunately have disappeared.

In 1334 Giotto was given the important post of *capomaestro* (superintendent of works) of the Commune of Florence and of the cathedral. The document that assigned him responsibility for the city's walls, fortifications, and other communal projects declares that he "should be welcomed as a great master in his native land and should be held dear" there, a singular honor for an artist of the time. What exactly Giotto did during his tenure as *capomaestro* is uncertain, but it seems likely that he designed the campanile (the free-standing bell tower of the cathedral).

In 1335 Giotto's name appears in a legal record, and that prosaic notice is the last one hears of him before his death in 1337. The contemporary Florentine chronicler Giovanni Villani writes that Giotto died after a trip to Milan and that he was buried with great honors in the cathedral he helped to build. Such a distinction, which was usually reserved for prelates, statesmen, and soldiers, demonstrates the high esteem in which Giotto was held by his fellow Florentines.

Giotto's fresco cycle in the Scrovegni Chapel remains a major monument in the history of Western art. It is one of the earliest and largest painted fresco cycles of the early Renaissance. The organization of its narratives into registers of subtly interrelated stories set between a ceiling and a lower level fundamentally influenced the design of painted chapels

Fig. 12. Giotto, *The Meeting at the Golden Gate* (c. 1305), Scrovegni Chapel, Padua (see pl. 6)

throughout the Renaissance. It is also an early landmark in the history of the design, technique, and execution of a fresco, a medium that was to become so essential in the Italian Renaissance. The impact of the Scrovegni Chapel frescoes was felt not only in Padua, but throughout Northern Italy; they immediately helped to transform the style and interpretation of generations of native artists.

Perhaps the most important and lasting contribution of Giotto's work in the Scrovegni Chapel is his lucid interpretation of religious drama that continually emphasizes universal human feelings both in the individual stories and through the unfolding narrative sequence on the chapels walls. Seldom in the history of art has such a complex narrative cycle been presented with such sustained clarity, directness, and empathy.

Giotto's ability to interrelate and weave together both form and meaning through the many frescoes is both skillful and uncanny.

This brilliant interpretation was revolutionary and immensely influential, because for the first time, holy figures were depicted with all the strengths and frailties of the worshipper. Christ, His mother, His followers, and sometimes His enemies are, in many ways, each of us. No longer symbolic abstractions, they are men and women with real, often conflicting, human emotions, who, through their tribulations and triumphs, convey a luminous and eternal message of abiding hope. Realized through the power of his magisterial and innovative genius, Giotto's transcendent vision in paint is as compelling and moving today as it was when the frescoes were new well over half a millennium ago.

Notes

1. Dante identified Riginaldo using the pregnant sow on his coat of arms, the same animal seen on Enrico's tomb (see fig. 5). See *The Divine Comedy: Hell* (trans. D. Sayers), Harmondsworth, 1964, p. 176. Riginaldo's last words were said to have been, "Give me the keys to my strong box so that no one may get my money." It has been suggested, and widely believed, that the frescoes in the Scrovegni Chapel have references to ursury—see especially U. Schlegel, "On the Picture Program of the Arena Chapel," in *Giotto: The Arena Chapel Frescoes* (ed. J. Stubblebine), New York, 1969, pp. 182–202. Although scenes of commerce and money and the depiction of money bags (in *The Cleansing of the Temple*, in *The Pact of Judas*, and in *The Last Judgment*) appear in the chapel, they are simply parts of the canonical sequence of the Christian drama without, as far as one can see, any specific reference to contemporary ursury. Why, in any case, would Enrico Scrovegni want to call attention to this dubious family activity? In his book on Padua in the early fourteenth century, J. Hyde says, "Enrico Scrovegni's building of the famous Arena Chapel...may have been intended in part to expiate the sins of his father, but there is nothing to suggest this, even in the attacks on Enrico's character made by Da Nono [Giovanni da Nono, a contemporary historian] and the friars of the Eremitani, both of which concentrate on his hypocrisy and vainglory." See J. Hyde, *Padua in the Age of Dante*, Manchester, 1966, p. 190.

2. This document, in the Archivio Comunale of Padua, is translated in *Giotto: The Arena Chapel Frescoes* (ed. J. Stubblebine), New York, 1969, pp. 106–7.

3. On the Virgin of Charity and the Scrovegni Chapel, see D. Shorr, "The Role of the Virgin in Giotto's *Last Judgment*," *The Art Bulletin* 38 (1956): 207–14.

4. This document, in the Vatican archives, is translated in *Giotto: The Arena Chapel Frescoes* (ed. J. Stubblebine), New York, 1969, p. 105.

Selected Bibliography

Renaissance History

Brucker, G., *Renaissance Florence*, Berkeley, 1983. (A concise, lucid introduction.)

Burckhardt, J., *The Civilization of the Renaissance in Italy*, New York, 1958. (First published in 1860, but still the classic and seminal historical formulation of the Renaissance.)

Burke, P., *The Italian Renaissance; Culture and Society in Italy*, Princeton, 1986. (Much valuable material; especially good on patronage.)

Hyde, J., *Padua in the Age of Dante*, Manchester, 1966. (Informative study of the governing class around the time of the Scrovegni Chapel.)

Larner, J., *Culture and Society in Italy 1290–1420*, London, 1971. (Much interesting information on artists and art of the period.)

History of Renaissance Art

Cole, B., *Italian Art 1250–1550: The Relation between Renaissance Art and Society*, New York, 1987. (Discusses art by type and function.)

Freedberg, S., *Painting in Italy 1500–1600*, Harmondsworth, 1975. (Magisterial, definitive study of later Renaissance painting.)

Hartt, F., *History of Renaissance Art*, New York, 1987. (Perceptive survey.)

Pope-Hennessy, J., *Italian Gothic Sculpture*, London; *Italian Renaissance Sculpture*, New York, 1985. (The definitive histories.)

White, J., *Art and Architecture in Italy 1250–1400*, Harmondsworth, 1987. (Important, often provocative study of the early Renaissance.)

Renaissance Frescoes

Borsook, E., *The Mural Painters of Tuscany*, Oxford, 1980. (Comprehensive survey of fresco painting in the Renaissance.)

Cole, B., *The Renaissance Artist at Work*, New York, 1983. (Discusses the training and working methods of Renaissance artists.)

Giotto

Cole, B., *Giotto and Florentine Painting 1280–1375*, New York, 1976. (Introduction to Giotto and his artistic contemporaries.)

Martindale, A., and E. Bacchesci, *The Complete Painting of Giotto*, New York, 1966. (Valuable for its many photographs.)

Salvini, R., *Giotto bibliografia*, Rome, 1938; C. de Benedictis, *Giotto bibliografia*, vol. II, Rome, 1973. (Splendid bibliographies; indispensable for study.)

Glossary of Fresco Terms

Affresco (in English usage, "fresco"). Painting with pigments dissolved in water on freshly laid plaster. As both plaster and paint dry, they become completely integrated. Known as the "true" fresco (or *buon* fresco), this technique was most popular from the late thirteenth to the mid-sixteenth centuries.

Arriccio. The preliminary layer of plaster spread on the masonry. The sinopia is executed on this layer. The *arriccio* was left rough so that the final, top layer (see *intonaco*) might more easily adhere to it.

Cartone (in English usage, "cartoon"). The artist's final drawing on paper or cloth of the main lines of the composition; it is sometimes, but not always, equal in size to the wall area to be painted. (Several cartoons might be used to create one large image.) The cartoon was laid against the wall over the final, freshly laid plaster on which the artist would paint. Its outlines were incised on the plaster by pressure from a stylus to guide the artist in painting. This procedure was common in the sixteenth century. The *spolvero* technique (see below) was commonly used as well.

Giornata. The patch of *intonaco* to be painted "daily," not necessarily in one day. The artist decided in advance the size of the surface he would paint and laid on top of the *arriccio* only the amount of fresh *intonaco* needed for his work. The joinings are usually discernible upon a close examination of the painted surface, and they disclose the order in which the patches were painted, because each successive patch slightly overlaps the preceding one.

Intonaco. The final, smooth layer of plaster for the finished painting. It was made from lime and sand and laid in sections.

Mezzo fresco. Painting on partially dry plaster. The pigment penetrates the plaster less deeply than with the "true" fresco method, and the carbonation is less extensive. *Mezzo* fresco was a popular procedure in the sixteenth and later centuries.

Pontata. *Intonaco* spread in wide bands that correspond to successively lower stages of the scaffold. The painter frequently laid some preparatory colors on these large surfaces as they were drying, but he usually spread his final colors after the *intonaco* had dried. This is largely, then, a *secco* technique.

Secco (literally, "dry"). Painting on plaster that has already dried. The colors are mixed with an adhesive or binder to attach them to the surface to be painted. The binding medium may be made from various substances, such as tempera. Tempera (the addition of egg yolk to pigments) was commonly used to complete a composition already painted in fresco. Because the pigment and the dry wall surface do not become thoroughly united, as they do in "true" fresco, *secco* mural paintings tend to deteriorate and flake off the walls more rapidly.

Sinopia. Originally a red ochre named after Sinope, a town on the Black Sea that was well known for its red pigments. In fresco technique the term is used for the final preparatory drawing on the *arriccio*, which was normally executed in red ochre.

Spolvero. An early method (see *cartone*) of transferring the artist's drawing onto the *intonaco*. After drawings as large as the frescoes were made on paper, their outlines were pricked, and the paper was cut into pieces the size of each day's work. After the day's patch of *intonaco* was laid, the corresponding drawing was placed over it and "dusted" with a cloth sack filled with charcoal powder, which passed through the tiny punctured holes to mark the design on the wall. This method was most popular in the second half of the fifteenth century.

Stacco. The process of detaching a fresco painting from the wall by removing the pigment and the *intonaco*. Usually an animal glue is applied to the painted surface and then two layers of cloth (calico and canvas) are applied, left to dry, and later stripped off the wall, pulling the fresco with them. It is taken to a laboratory, where the excess plaster is scraped away and another cloth is attached to its back. Finally, the cloths on the face of the fresco are carefully removed. The fresco is then ready to be mounted on a new support.

Strappo. The process by which a fresco is detached from a wall when the plaster on which it is painted has greatly deteriorated. *Strappo* takes off only the color layer with very small amounts of plaster. It is effected by the use of a glue considerably stronger than that used in the *stacco* technique, but the procedure that follows is identical. After certain frescoes are removed by the means of *strappo*, a colored imprint may still be seen on the plaster remaining on the wall. This is evidence of the depth to which the pigment penetrated the plaster. These traces of color are often removed by a second *strappo* operation on the same wall.

View facing entrance wall of the Scrovegni Chapel

Plates and Commentaries

*In reproducing the individual frescoes of the Scrovegni Chapel,
we have preserved a sense of their orientation to the chancel
arch, so that those to its right are reproduced on a
right-hand page in this volume and those to its left
are reproduced on a left-hand page here.*

1. *The Expulsion of Joachim from the Temple*

In the Scrovegni Chapel, Giotto creates figures whose volume and weight are without precedent. Firmly rooted to the ground, serious of purpose, and often heroic, they are real presences whose bodies express clearly and forcefully their particular roles in the stories. Each figure acts within a spatial framework of remarkable clarity and economy. With these figures and this space, Giotto developed a new, expressive realism that probes the physical and psychological core of each story he painted. In *The Expulsion of Joachim from the Temple* and in almost every other fresco in the Scrovegni Chapel, he does not simply accept the traditional, time-honored representational conventions of religious narrative of his day. Instead he ponders anew the meaning of each story. Giotto's pictorial style and his interpretation of drama revolutionized painting in the Italian peninsula. His work was a source of inspiration and instruction for generations of painters; it was studied and absorbed by Masaccio, Leonardo da Vinci, Michelangelo, and Raphael, artists whose own work was to be of such fundamental importance for the history of European art.

The fictive marble seen here in the temple and throughout the narrative frescoes and decoration in the Scrovegni Chapel was made by an ancient painting technique. The pigments were mixed with some sort of saponified oil, and then, after application, the surface was pressed with a hot iron. This process created a smooth, durable, and highly realistic portrayal of veined marble.

The narrative frescoes on the side walls of the Scrovegni Chapel, except for those flanked by windows, are framed with painted borders. In the middle of these bands of geometric and floral ornament are quatrefoils (four-lobed decorative shapes) containing either a single bust-length figure or small scene. The identity of some of these figures is problematic, but several of the scenes are related to the adjacent story, usually as Old Testament prefigurations.

2. *Joachim among the Shepherds*

Ashamed to go home after his expulsion from the temple, the dejected Joachim returns to his sheepfold. The drama is compressed and concentrated by the stage set–like hill that, except at the far right behind the little hut, never rises much above the middle of the painting. All of the figures are kept below the crest of the hill, whose barren, flinty nature reflects Joachim's spiritual desperation. Such expressive landscape elements are frequently used by Giotto in the Scrovegni Chapel. Joachim's despondency is communicated by his bent head and by the knowing glances of the two shepherds. Even Joachim's little dog, sensing that something is very wrong, seems to hesitate in mid-leap.

3. *The Annunciation to St. Anne*

Anne, Joachim's wife, is extremely worried when he does not return from the temple. While she weeps over her husband's absence, an angel appears and announces to her that she will, at long last, bear a child, who is to be named Mary. Giotto has omitted the front wall of the simple house so as to reveal the Annunciation. To the left is a porch that serves as the architectural and spatial threshold to the miracle. Here the young woman intent on her spinning seems to sense that something momentous is occurring behind the closed door. Even though Joachim was a wealthy man, Giotto has made the house and its furnishings meager to reflect Anne's humbleness: for Giotto, plainness and simplicity were equivalents of virtue and purity.

4. *Joachim's Sacrifice*

The scene shifts back to the inhospitable terrain of Joachim's sheepfold: the rocky outcrop seen at the right of *Joachim among the Shepherds* is echoed here by a nearly identical crag. However, now the action is directed upward, toward the small altar set on the top of the hill, where Joachim makes his own personal sacrifice to God. Unlike the static, depressing background of *Joachim among the Shepherds*, the undulating landscape here seems to energize the action. As the sacrificial sheep still burns on the altar, the hand of God appears in the sky to bless Joachim and accept his offering.

5. *The Dream of Joachim*

After he has made his sacrificial offering, Joachim dreams of an angel, who appears in a blaze of light to announce that Joachim's wife, Anne, will bear a child. This will be Mary, who "as she will be born of a barren mother, so will she herself, in wondrous wise, beget the Son of the Most High, Whose name will be called Jesus, and through Whom salvation will come to all nations!"* The angel then tells Joachim to go to the Golden Gate in Jerusalem, where he will met a joyful Anne.

Here the rocky landscape of the sheepfold appears once again, albeit in slightly modified form. The slope of the hill in the background seems both to echo and convey the message of the flying angel. Although this is Joachim's dream, the two shepherds, and even Joachim's dog, seem to sense the divine presence in the sky.

*The Golden Legend (trans. G. Ryan and H. Rippeger), New York, 1969, pp. 522–23.

6. *The Meeting at the Golden Gate*

Joachim and Anne follow the angel's directive to go to the Golden Gate in Jerusalem. Here they are reunited for the first time since Joachim left home to take his sacrifice to the temple; they now share the joyous knowledge of the impending birth of their child, an event that will alter their lives forever. This fresco, which ends the opening register of the Scrovegni Chapel, is one of great tenderness. There has been much guesswork, but little agreement, about the identity of the woman in black, the only truly ambiguous figure in the Scrovegni Chapel. Unlike the happy, gawking women, she looks away from the private and intimate embrace of Joachim and Anne.

7. The Birth of the Virgin

After their meeting at the Golden Gate, Joachim and Anne returned home to await the birth of Mary as foretold by the angel. In this fresco, the action takes place in the couple's home, the same house in which Anne received the Annunciation. Giotto, unlike most artists before him, is particularly interested in the sequence of narrative events through time and space; consequently, he replicates with great care the settings that are the scenes of several stories in the Scrovegni Chapel.

The Birth of the Virgin is a crowded, homey scene filled with the bustle and happiness of birth. Mary appears twice. In the foreground, immediately after delivery, her eyes are washed and she is wrapped in swaddling clothes. Only then is she presented to Anne, who eagerly reaches out to embrace her new baby for the first time. This double representation of a figure in the same time and space frame is unusual for Giotto, but quite common in earlier painting.

Giotto had assistants working with him in the Scrovegni Chapel, but the style of the paintings is, nonetheless, remarkably uniform. Only occasionally, as in the rather poorly drawn women tending Mary, may small parts of individual frescoes be attributed to the hands of helpers.

8. *The Presentation of the Virgin*

When she was three years old, the Virgin was brought to the temple. To the amazement of all, she climbed the fifteen steps up to the building alone—Giotto, who often modifies the details of a story, depicts only ten steps. The temple is the same structure seen in *The Expulsion of Joachim from the Temple*; here, however, it is viewed from what appears to be the front, with the tabernacle and the pulpit with the staircase seen from the opposite side. But instead of a place of spiritual and physical rejection, the temple is now the location of a tender scene of welcoming and acceptance. Mary is poised between the supportive arms of her mother and the welcoming gesture of the high priest. The haloed figure at the left is almost certainly Joseph, the future husband of Mary.

9. *The Virgin's Suitors Presenting Their Rods*

In her fourteenth year, the Virgin left the temple to be married. The Jewish elders prayed for guidance in this matter, and when, according to *The Golden Legend*, Zacharias went into the temple to pray, a voice told him "that the marriageable men of the house of David who had not yet taken a wife, each should bring a dry branch and lay it upon the altar."* The suitor whose rod flowered would be the one chosen to marry the Virgin. The old Joseph was one of these men, but at first he offered no rod for "it seemed not fitting that a man of his years

should take so young a maid to wife, so that when all the others placed branches upon the altar, he alone left none."** In this scene we see the reticent Joseph at the far left looking on as the eager young men present their rods to the high priest. This is a new temple seen in a cutaway form that reveals its nave, altar, and side aisles. Its form is not unlike a typical church of Giotto's time.

The Golden Legend, p. 524.
**The Golden Legend*, p. 524.

10. *The Suitors' Prayer before the Rods*

In the same temple seen in the last fresco, the rods, including the one that Joseph has unwillingly placed among the others, have been set upon the altar before which the suitors and priests await the miraculous blooming. All the figures are confined to the lower third of the painting, with the young suitors packed closely together in the lower left corner. Here, once again, Joseph's reticence is underscored by the appearance of only his haloed head at the extreme left. The compression of the figures and the expectant attitudes of their kneeling bodies transmit a strong sense of anticipation and hope. Giotto chose to convey the high dramatic tension of anticipation, rather than the miraculous flowering of the rod itself. The eventual blooming of Joseph's dry rod is often seen as a symbol of resurrection, which is most appropriate considering the sepulchral function of the Scrovegni Chapel.

11. *The Marriage of the Virgin*

The marriage of the Virgin and Joseph takes place in the temple seen in the previous two frescoes. Here the action is strung across the painting by the frieze-like disposition of the standing figures. At the left are the disappointed suitors, one of whom breaks his rod across his knee in frustration. Near the middle of the fresco, a smiling man is about to give Joseph a congratulatory slap on the back. A much calmer atmosphere pervades the interior of the temple, where the marriage takes place. The figures of Mary, Joseph, the high priest, and the spectators are all nestled within the apse, whose curved dome is echoed by their gently inclining bodies. Joseph holds the sign of God's blessing, the flowering rod, upon which the Holy Spirit has alighted. The lily that blooms from the rod is often used as a symbol of Mary's purity.

12. *The Virgin's Wedding Procession*

There has been debate about the subject of this fresco. Some scholars believe that it depicts the Virgin returning to the temple after her marriage. Others suggest that it shows the Virgin returning to her parents' house in Galilee, or perhaps the Virgin going to her new home with Joseph. The latter interpretation seems most correct, because the procession moves toward, and is adjacent to, *The Annunciation* on the chancel arch in which both the angel and the Virgin are seen in the latter's house. *The Virgin's Wedding Procession* is notable for its beautifully elongated figures disposed in a rhythmic frieze across the surface. There is a dance-like tenor here that accords perfectly with what one imagines are the dulcet sounds of the musicians' instruments. The prominent leafing branch protruding from the balcony is surely an illusion to the Virgin's forthcoming pregnancy.

Much of the upper half of the fresco has been badly damaged. A wooden grate has been barbarously set into the right side of the narrative, destroying a considerable amount of paint.

Note: The area above the altar (marked "13" on the diagram of the Scrovegni Chapel painting program reproduced on page 26 of this volume) shows *God the Father Dispatching Gabriel.*

The Annunciation

14a. The Angel Gabriel

Because one of the Scrovegni
Chapel's dedications was to
the Annunciation to the Virgin,
these two frescoes take on special
significance. They are immediately
visible as one enters the chapel,
and they are the only large paintings
occupied by just a single figure.
The Incarnation of Christ took
place as the angel Gabriel said to
the Virgin: "Fear not, Mary, for
thou hast found grace with God.
Behold thou shalt bring forth a
Son, and thou shalt call his name
Jesus (that is, Savior), for He shall
save His people from their sins."*
This was the first act of mankind's
salvation. So important was this
event that the feast day of the
Annunciation on March 25
(exactly nine months before
Christ's birth) was also the beginning of the new year in many
Italian communes.

*The Golden Legend, p. 205.

14b. The Virgin

The Annunciation was also extremely relevant because the chapel served as the burial place for the Scrovegni family, who would have taken comfort in the redeeming power of the Incarnation as expressed in Gabriel's words.

The two rooms in which the Annunciation occurs are mirror images of each other, and the angel's message seems to be conveyed along the chancel arch itself. Each of the large, handsome figures is surrounded by an aura of divine light.

15. *The Visitation*

Standing outside a porch (a device Giotto often uses to signal an important transitional event), the Virgin and St. Elizabeth embrace. Both women are pregnant—the Virgin with Christ and Elizabeth with St. John the Baptist. Like the Virgin's mother, Anne, Elizabeth was old and barren when the miraculous birth of a son was announced to her husband, Zacharias, by the angel Gabriel. The placement of this fresco directly under that of the Virgin of the Annunciation further amplifies the importance of the Annunciation for the Scrovegni Chapel. Even though the Virgin is the younger woman, Elizabeth bows respectfully as a sign of deference to Mary's holiness.

The colors of this fresco—light green, red, mustard yellow, and blue—are beautifully placed across the surface. Almost all of the blue originally applied dry *(secco)* to the robe of the attendant behind Elizabeth has fallen off the wall, revealing the sinopia underneath but depriving the scene of the strong note of color that would have closed the right side of the composition. The harmony and serenity of this fresco make a strong contrast to the perfidiousness of *The Pact of Judas* directly across the chancel arch.

16. *The Nativity*

Next to *The Visitation* on the chancel arch is *The Nativity*, the first fresco of the middle register of the right wall. The detailed, homey nature of the *Meditations on the Life of Christ*, one of the principal textual sources influenced Giotto's conception of this story:

> At midnight on Sunday, when the hour of birth came, the Virgin rose and stood erect against a column that was there. But Joseph remained seated, downcast perhaps because he could not prepare what was necessary. Then he rose and, taking some hay from the manger, placed it at the Lady's feet and turned away. The Son of the eternal God came out of the womb of the mother without a murmur or lesion, in a moment; as He had been in the womb so He was now outside, on the hay at His mother's feet. Unable to contain herself, the mother stooped to pick Him up, embraced Him tenderly and, guided by the Holy Spirit, placed Him in her lap and began to wash Him with her milk, her breast filled by heaven. When this was done, she wrapped Him in the veil from her head and laid Him in the manger. The ox and the ass knelt with their mouths above the manger and breathed on the Infant as though they possessed reason and knew that the Child was so poorly wrapped that He needed to be warmed, in that cold season.*

Meditations on the Life of Christ (trans. I. Ragusa and R. Green), Princeton, 1977, pp. 32–34.

17. *The Adoration of the Magi*

In this, one of the most splendid and joyous frescoes in the Scrovegni Chapel, the three Magi adore the Child. These men were Eastern astrologers who saw signs in the heavens of the birth of Christ. Below a blazing star, these wise men stare in reverent wonder at the Christ Child. The oldest of the group kneels to kiss the feet of the infant tenderly, as an angel holding one of the Magi's golden gifts looks on. This gift resembles a monstrance, a liturgical vessel in which the Eucharistic Host (the symbolic body of Christ) is displayed—the parallel between this gift and the presentation of the infant Christ to the Magi is clear. The exotic origins of the Magi are indicated by the alert, blue-eyed camels held by attentive members of their retinue.

Giotto has painted this fresco with many luminous, light colors punctuated by notes of red that help to create the glowing mood of the story. All of the figures and animals in this painting are particularly well preserved, except for the Virgin's blue mantel, which has fallen away, revealing a sketchy sinopia drawing beneath.

18. *The Presentation of Christt*

According to Mosaic law, Jesus was brought to the temple to be presented to God. Two turtle-doves were also brought for the rite of the purification of the mother after birth—these are held by Joseph, who stands behind the Virgin. It had been divinely revealed to the aged priest Simeon, who holds the Child, that he would not die until he had seen the Messiah. When he saw Christ he said, "Lord, now lettest thou thy servant depart in peace according to thy word; for mine eyes have seen thy salvation which thou hast prepared in the presence of all peoples, a light for revelation to the Gentiles, and a glory to thy people Israel." (Luke 2:29–32) Again, the emphasis on salvation would be understood as a reference to the chapel's sepulchral function.

At the far right of the scene, the old prophetess Anna indicates the Child as Savior. The embroiered altar cloth seen in *The Virgin's Suitors Presenting Their Rods* and *The Suitors' Prayer before the Rods* reappears here. Especially charming and human is Giotto's depiction of Christ as a frightened infant who reaches out for his mother.

19. *The Flight into Egypt*

An angel appeared to Joseph in a dream and told him to flee with his family to Egypt. There he would avoid Herod's men, who were seeking to kill Christ. In this fresco, the little group of the Virgin, Christ, Joseph, and four attendants are guided by an angel. The subject of this painting is flight, and Giotto has imbued his composition with a sense of urgency. Behind the foreground figures, the hill itself, which echoes the triangular shape of the mother and Child riding the donkey, appears to move toward the right, the direction in which the figures hurry. The sense of movement is further underscored by the staccato drumbeat of the fleeing feet marching along the narrow ledge. Joseph, leading the way, turns back as if to prod the group on to greater speed.

The entire color balance of this painting has been seriously disturbed by the loss of the bright blue of the Virgin's mantle at the very center of the composition.

20. *The Massacre of the Innocents*

Hearing from the Magi that Christ would become king of the Jews, Herod Ascalon, the tetrarch of Galilee, sent his soldiers to kill all the children of Bethlehem under two years of age. In the fresco, the two building types in the background would have been recognized by Giotto's contemporaries. At the left is a communal building, perhaps a town hall with a balcony for speeches; at the right is a baptistery—such baptisteries were often free-standing. In front of the baptistery, which here serves as a symbol of the infants' entry into the church, the mothers strive in vain to save their children. From the balcony of the neighboring building, a symbol of the state, Herod urges on his murderous troops. The actual killing is done by three men, one seen from behind. The executioners' once-gold swords have since flaked off the wall.

The faces of the other two murderers are bestial—Giotto's abiding faith in the goodness of human beings did not permit him to paint normal-looking men carrying out such a heinous deed. This deep faith also allowed him to reinterpret the roles of the soldiers at the far left of the painting daringly. Instead of mindlessly participating in the massacre, they are horrified by it. In fact, their flight toward the left, contrary to the normal directional flow of the Scrovegni Chapel frescoes, demonstrates their revulsion. The pile of dead babies stacked like cordwood is disturbingly familiar to our own time.

21. *Christ among the Doctors*

While visiting Jerusalem for the Feast of
Passover, the`twelve-year-old Jesus, unbe-
knownst to His parents, visited Solomon's Temple.
There He engaged in a discussion so learned that the
elders of the temple were astonished by His knowledge. The Virgin and Joseph, frantic with worry,
finally found Him among the wise men and
implored Him to return to Bethlehem.

      The painting of *Christ among the Doctors* is
badly damaged and was, moreover, repainted, probably in the nineteenth century. This is unfortunate
because it is one of the most ambitious frescoes in
the chapel. In no other painting in the cycle is there
such a large and complex interior architectural setting. There is also an unusually deep spatial recession
created by the semicircle of doctors surrounding
Christ.

22. *The Baptism of Christ*

Christ was baptized by John the Baptist in the Jordan River before a great crowd. During the baptism, Christ "saw the heavens opened and the Spirit descending upon Him like a dove; and a voice came from heaven, 'thou art my beloved Son; and with thee I am well pleased.'" (Mark 1:10–11) Directly above Christ's head, the foreshortened figure of God appears in a burst of divine radiance that seems to have cleaved the mountains. The act of baptism, here shown without John pouring water over Christ's head, is the riveting focus of attention for Christ's followers and for the magnificent angels who hold His robes. Seldom in the history of art has this scene of minimal action been turned into such compelling drama.

Here, as in many other frescoes in the Scrovegni Chapel, some of the halos, usually those of the figures nearest the observer, are made of built-up plaster that was scored and then gilded with a mixture of copper, silver, gold, and lead. In some frescoes, this amalgam has oxidized, turning the halos black. Here, however, they have fortunately retained their original color.

23. *The Wedding at Cana*

Christ and the Virgin were invited to a wedding feast at Cana, a city in Galilee (according to several ancient legends, John the Evangelist was the bridegroom). During the festivities, the wine ran out and the Virgin implored Christ to help. He ordered six jugs filled with water, which He then miraculously changed to wine. This was Christ's first miracle and a foreshadowing of the transubstantiation of His blood into the Eucharistic wine. The miracle is not yet apparent to all, for the wine steward, whose potbelly humorously resembles the water jugs, is just tasting the wine, which all would deem the finest they had ever drunk. In the fashion of the fourteenth century, the guests are seated on only one side of the table, so that the servants may hand the food and drink from the front.

The quatrefoil depicts *Moses Drawing Water from the Rock*. This miracle, which he performed to quench the thirst of his followers in the desert, is here seen as foreshadowing Christ's transformation of water into wine at Cana. Moses' act was also an Old Testament parallel for Christ as a spring of spiritual rejuvenation for His followers.

.

24. *The Raising of Lazarus*

Mary Magdalene and Martha, friends of Christ, urged Him to come to Bethany to cure their sick brother Lazarus, but He did not come at once. By the time He arrived, Lazarus had been dead for four days. The sisters implored Christ to bring their brother back to life. Christ told Martha that her brother would rise again. His words were: "I am the resurrection and the life; he who believes in me, though he die, yet shall he live, and whomever lives and believes in me shall never die." (John 11:25–26) Given the sepulchral nature of the Scrovegni Chapel, Christ's words have a particularly pointed meaning here.

The scene revolves around Christ's miracle-working hand, which appears isolated in the void between His followers and the men surrounding Lazarus, some of whom cover their noses against the stench of decomposition. From this hand the divine spark of resurrection seems to speed through the outstretched arm next to it, then down through the body of the man holding Lazarus. All this has happened so suddenly that Mary and Martha are unaware of Lazarus's resurrection, as the prostrate pair still implore Christ to raise their brother. The blooming trees and the lily on the otherwise barren mountain are symbols of God's regenerative power, a force that will also resurrect Christ himself.

In the quatrefoil is *The Creation of Adam*, an earlier act of divine life-giving. Like Adam, Christ, who was often called the Second Adam, was the first man of his era. Christ was, moreover, sent to earth to redeem mankind from Adam's sin.

25. *The Entry into Jerusalem*

The composition of this scene, the first episode of Christ's Passion, recalls *The Flight into Egypt*, but the meanings of the two stories are very different indeed. In *The Flight into Egypt* Christ and his family flee from death, but in *The Entry into Jerusalem* Christ stoically begins the process that will lead inexorably to His capture, humiliation, and eventual Crucifixion. Making a gesture much like the one He makes in the previous scene, *The Raising of Lazarus*, He rides toward the Golden Gate of Jerusalem, where throngs of adoring citizens acclaim him. The rowdy crowds pouring out of the narrow gate—a variation on the structure seen in *The Meeting at the Golden Gate*—contrast strongly with the calm, orderly group of Christ's followers. Especially interesting is the sequential, almost cinematic action of the three men in the right foreground: one begins to pull off his robe, another has his robe over his head, and the third lays his robe under the feet of Christ's donkey. Further excitement is created by the man climbing the tree to get a glimpse of the famous preacher and miracle worker. Another man gathers palm fronds, a symbol of martyrdom—the boy in front of Christ's donkey holds up a frond.

26. *The Cleansing of the Temple*

In front of the temple porch, Christ uses a whip to drive out the money changers, merchants, and animal sellers who have defiled the sacred area by setting up shop there. The animals were sold for sacrifice in the temple: sheep for wealthy people, and pigeons for the poor. This fresco has been badly damaged by the loss of much pigment put in *secco*. The blue of Christ's robe has fallen off, revealing sinopia drawings. This large area of blue would have been the focal point of the composition. Christ's violent gesture, his stern face, the bolting goats, and the flight of the merchants all create a strong and swift rightward movement toward the next scene, *The Pact of Judas,* where the priests, reacting to Christ's behavior in front of the temple, plot to have Him killed. Originally, the now badly damaged legs and supports of the overturned counting table in front of Christ would have intensified the strong horizontal movement in this area of the fresco.

Giotto was a masterful, sure artist, but occasionally he changed his mind about a painting. After he had finished the St. Peter to the immediate left of Christ, he decided to put in a figure of a boy, perhaps to make Peter a less isolated shape. He cut out a section below Peter's waist, laid in a new patch of plaster, and then covered it with the boy's head. The rest of the boy's body, like the blue of Christ's robe, was painted in *secco* and has since fallen off, revealing the underlying yellow over which it was painted and further disturbing the original color harmony of the fresco.

In the quatrefoil, the Archangel Michael cleanses heaven by vanquishing Satan. Christ's expulsion of the money changers from the temple is a similar triumph of good over evil.

27. The Pact of Judas

As he does with the temples seen in several of the frescoes, Giotto duplicates important characters who reappear throughout the cycle. An example of this is found in *The Pact of Judas* on the chancel arch, where the three priests seen at the extreme right of *The Cleansing of the Temple* appear once again. Two of the them discuss Judas's perfidy, while the third plots with Judas, who is firmly in the grip of the devil. This fresco makes a strong spiritual and moral contrast to *The Visitation* on the other side of the chancel arch. Their compositions are alike—each has a similar architectural setting and contains five figures—but their meanings could not be more dissimilar.

28. *The Last Supper*

Christ and his followers are seen celebrating the Feast of Passover in a room on the upper floor of a house in Jerusalem. There are two essential elements to this story. First, it is here that the institution of the Eucharistic ritual is established and the first communion of the apostles taken:

> *Now as they were eating, Jesus took bread,*
> *and blessed, and broke it, and gave it to the disciples*
> *and said, 'Take, eat; this is my body.' And He took a*
> *cup, and when He had given thanks He gave it to*
> *them saying, 'Drink of it, all of you; for this is my*
> *blood of the covenant, which is poured out for many*
> *for the forgiveness of sins.' (Matthew 26:26–28)*

This fresco, the first on the lowest right register, is the one closest to the altar at which the priest would perform the central ritual of the Mass with its Eucharistic symbolism. Closest to the altar on the left side is *The Pentecost*, the miracle that established the Christian Church. Both frescoes make an apt metaphorical and liturgical frame for the altar.

The second key element of the story is a historical one. It was at the Last Supper that Christ announced that one of the apostles would betray Him: "He who has dipped his hand in the dish with me, will betray me." (Matthew 26:23) Judas, wearing the same yellow robe he wore in *The Pact of Judas*, dips his hand in the bowl, knowing that he will soon betray Christ.

29. *The Washing of the Feet*

When the Last Supper was finished, Christ stood up, wrapped a towel around His waist, and began to wash the feet of the apostles. Peter, whose feet Christ here is about to wash, protested what he considered to be a humiliating act on Christ's part. The trestle table has been removed, but otherwise the room is exactly the same as it was in the previous scene, *The Last Supper*. Originally there were geometric wall decorations behind the apostles, but almost all of these have flaked off the wall.

The Scrovegni Chapel is illuminated by five windows in the right wall, but the painted light in the frescoes does not come from the direction of them. Rather, it seems to emanate from the entrance wall, with its large figure of Christ at the center of *The Last Judgment*. The painted light flows from a divine source, not a mundane one. This is clear in *The Washing of the Feet*, where the light, seemingly originating from the direction of the entrance wall, strikes the right sides of the figures.

30. *The Betrayal of Christ*

Judas was to identify Christ by a kiss, an act of friendship he would turn into betrayal. Here Giotto, unlike most artists before him, has chosen not to portray the moment of the kiss, but the split second after the betrayal. The soldiers have already surrounded Christ, entrapping Him in the iron ring of their dark helmets. In a fit of anger over Christ's capture, Peter cuts off the ear of Malchus, the servant of the high priest. At the left of the composition, the apostles try to flee—one of their robes is held by a faceless enemy. This leftward movement is a departure from the usual left-to-right direction found throughout the chapel. In the crowd at the far right, the evil priest seen in *The Cleansing of the Temple* reappears.

In the center of the maelstrom, as in the calm of a hurricane's eye, are Christ and Judas. Christ's body is nearly obliterated by the yellow robe worn by Judas. The two faces of betrayer and betrayed form the focal point of the story. Judas, realizing for the first time the enormity of his deed, draws back from the kiss in horror as his eyes meet Christ's steady, all-knowing gaze. This exchange, which could have been depicted only in the moment after the kiss, allows Giotto to reexamine the most complex human elements of the drama.

31. *Christ before Caiaphas*

After the betrayal by Judas, Christ was arrested and brought before the high priest Caiaphas for questioning. Caiaphas said to Christ, "I adjure you by the living God, tell us if you are the Christ, the Son of God." (Matthew 26:63) Christ answered: "You have said so. But I tell you, hereafter you will see the Son of man seated at the right hand of Power, and coming on the clouds of heaven." (Matthew 26:64) At this Caiaphas accused Christ of blasphemy. He then tore his robes and condemned Christ for declaring himself the Messiah, a crime punishable by death.

The scene is set in a small, crowded, dark room with shuttered windows. Christ stands surrounded, trapped by His enemies. The colors of the robes in this fresco are somber, and the spectrum of color is restricted in keeping with the dread events here depicted. Caiaphas has just given his verdict, and a soldier is about to strike Christ. Christ turns away from His accusers and looks back to the left, toward all the scenes of His childhood and miracles depicted in the Scrovegni Chapel. Christ accepts His fate, but the human part of His nature faces the coming martyrdom with fear.

32. *The Mocking of Christ*

After his condemnation by Caiaphas, Christ is mocked, beaten, and whipped. Here in the courtyard of a room with barred windows, the massive but enervated Christ is tormented by a group of particularly ugly and vicious men. Clad in a resplendent gold robe, He wears the crown of thorns and holds a reed scepter as He is mocked as the king of the Jews. One man kneels in false reverence, as the others pull Christ's hair and beat Him. Giotto, unlike other artists of this time, emphasized Christ's mortal nature by showing Him slumped and unconscious in the face of brutal torment.

The black man swinging the stick forms a transition between the group of Christ and his tormenters and the several figures to the far right.*

One of these, the man with the red robe and headband gesturing toward Christ, may be Pontius Pilate, the Roman governor of Judaea. Christ had been sent to Pilate because Caiaphas lacked the legal authority to sentence Him to death. Pilate felt that there was insufficient evidence for such a sentence, but because he feared the anger of the crowd, he washed his hands in front of the throng and then ordered Christ crucified, saying, "I am innocent of this man's blood; see to it yourselves." (Matthew 27:24)

*Giotto could have seen slaves in the homes of the wealthy in Florence and Padua.

33. *The Road to Calvary*

From the house of Pilate, Christ was forced to carry His cross to the hill of Golgotha, where He was crucified. Here a frieze of figures, led by Christ and His captors, moves across the fresco. Mary, the haloed figure on the far left, whose blue robe has flaked off the wall, is held back and prevented from following Christ. The gate from which the crowd exits is the third such structure in the Scrovegni Chapel: the others appear in *The Meeting at the Golden Gate* and *The Entry into Jerusalem*. In *The Meeting at the Golden Gate*, Joachim and one of his shepherds enter Jerusalem from the left and move toward the right. The same left-to-right movement is found in *The Entry into Jerusalem*. These gates are both placed on the right side of the paintings. In *The Road to Calvary*, however, Christ leads a procession that *leaves* a gate placed on the left side of the narrative. Moreover, this gate is the mirror image of the one He entered to begin His Passion. These changes in position and view of the gate bring both symmetry and closure to the harrowing events of the Passion sequence.

This fresco has been badly damaged. There is a general paint loss throughout, especially in the sky. Originally, the blue above the figures would have been enlivened by a series of diagonal shapes: a second cross to the right of Christ's and five tall lances held by the soldiers, all now only barely discernible.

34. *The Crucifixion*

The body of the crucified Christ, His head slumped in death on His chest, rises in isolation above the crowd. The cross separates the holy from the evil. To Christ's right, the good side, is the little group of the Virgin, John the Evangelist, and several other holy women. Mary Magdalene kneels at the base of the cross. She wipes the blood from Christ's feet, the same feet that, at Christ's Supper with Simon the Pharisee, she washed with her tears and dried with her hair (Luke 7:36–50). The Virgin, overcome by her son's death, faints into the arms of Christ's followers—once again the human, rather than the divine aspect of a holy figure, is stressed. On Christ's left, or sinister side, the soldiers fight over his seamless robe. Only the haloed soldier Longinus, who will later be martyred and revered as a saint, recognizes Christ's divinity.

Angels hover around the cross. One rends his garment in exactly the same way as does Caiaphas in the *Christ before Caiaphas* story on the right wall directly across from *The Crucifixion*—the death sentence Caiaphas set into motion is here executed. Three other angels gather Christ's blood into chalices. The redemptive power of this blood and of Christ's salvation of mankind from original sin is further emphasized by the skull of Adam seen below the cross.

35. *The Lamentation*

Christ has just been taken down from the cross and laid on the ground. His body links the mourners who have followed it from the cross to this rocky and barren place. Mary Magdalene sits in a state of numbed disbelief, caressing Christ's feet— the same feet she wiped with her own hair in *The Crucifixion*. John the Evangelist throws back his arms in grief, as the Virgin desperately searches Christ's face for some sign of life—is her left hand feeling for a pulse in His neck? Here the Virgin's embrace sadly recalls the way she held the Child in *The Nativity*. The two massive, boulder-like figures seen from behind form a perfect visual symbol of the weighty sorrow felt by Christ's followers. Behind Mary Magdalene is Joseph of Arimathaea, who has Christ's winding sheet draped around his neck like a prayer shawl; Joseph allowed Christ to be buried in his own sarcophagus, which can be glimpsed between Joseph of Arimathaea and John the Evangelist. At the far right is Nicodemus, who furnished spices for anointing Christ's body. A jagged, flinty rock outcropping capped by a dead tree adds a further barren note to this scene of despair.

This is one of the most auditory episodes in the Scrovegni Chapel. The mourners' wails reverberate through this stark landscape, mingling with the cries of sorrow and anger with which the contorted angels fill the heavens.

A scene of *Jonah Swallowed by the Whale* appears in the quatrefoil. After three days in the beast's belly, Jonah was regurgitated alive. This story of rebirth, often seen as foreshadowing the Resurrection of Christ, offers a small note of hope to the bleakness of the adjacent *Lamentation*.

36. *Noli Me Tangere*

The title of this story, *Noli Me Tangere* (Latin for "Don't Touch Me"), comes from Christ's admonition to Mary Magdalene after His Resurrection. Mary went to visit Christ's tomb and found it empty. There were two white angels where the body had been.

> They [the angels] said to her, "Woman, why are you weeping?" She said to them, "Because they have taken away my Lord, and I do not know where they have laid Him." Saying this, she turned round and saw Jesus standing, but she did not know that it was Jesus. Jesus said to her, "Woman, why are you weeping? Whom do you seek?" Supposing Him to be the gardener, she said to Him, "Sir, if you have carried Him away, tell me where you have laid Him, and I will take him away." Jesus said to her, "Mary." She turned and said to him ,"Rabboni!" (which means Teacher). Jesus said to her, "Do not hold me, for I have not yet ascended to the Father; but go to my brethren and say to them, I am ascending to my Father and your Father, to my God and your God." (John 20:13–17)

This scene follows *The Lamentation* and is closely tied to it by both the rocky outcropping, which seems to run through the two frescoes, and by Christ's sarcophagus, seen in both paintings. The lone dead tree that capped the summit of the stone ridge in *The Lamentation* is replaced here by blooming trees whose green foliage, unfortunately, has disappeared. Other plants seem miraculously to bloom where Christ steps.

The descending line of the outcropping leads to the focal point of the fresco: Christ's hand warding off the yearning Mary Magdalene, once again at His feet. Like the shining angels, Christ is dressed in a resplendent white garment trimmed with gold. As He gestures to Mary Magdalene, Christ begins to slip behind the right frame toward His Ascension, seen in the next fresco.

The quatrefoil depicts a lion with his cubs. During the Middle Ages, it was believed that lion cubs were born dead and that after three days their father brought them to life by breathing in their faces. This story is an apt analogue for Christ's Resurrection.

37. The Ascension

Forty days after His Resurrection, Christ ascended to heaven. Giotto has divided this fresco into the two realms of heaven and earth. Kneeling on the ground are the eleven apostles and the Virgin. These figures have been divided into two equal, tightly packed groups of six. Between them are two angels, who hover just above the ground. These heavenly figures form a smooth transition between the earth-bound apostles and the large figure of the ascending Christ. Surrounded by a glory of golden rays and clothed in a robe of dazzling white, He rises up to heaven on clouds. Flanking Him are two groups of flying angels, each placed above a group of apostles below.

Everything in this story is directed heavenward. The upturned heads of the apostles and angels, the path of their glances, the pointing hands of the hovering angels, and the swift flight of Christ's body are all ascendant. The heavenly part of the composition forms a triangle: the diagonally placed angel groups are at the sides, while Christ's head is at the apex; this shape directs and amplifies the upward movement. The usual horizontal, left-to-right direction of the Scrovegni Chapel narratives is no longer needed. Christ is now seen leaving the painting's worldly space at the very top of the fresco, as His outstretched hands slip beyond the upper border; His gaze is now directed upward, toward the enthroned figure of God at the top of the chancel arch.

This fresco is slightly mechanical in composition. Here, as in *The Last Judgment*, the necessity to include so many figures in so much of the fresco's space has become an obstacle to Giotto's usual concentrated and economical portrayal of drama.

A scene of *Elijah Ascending to Heaven in the Chariot of Fire* appears in the quatrefoil. This Old Testament story with its ascent into heaven was often seen as foreshadowing the Resurrection and Ascension of Christ.

38. *The Pentecost*

Ten days after the Ascension, the apostles were in Jerusalem celebrating the ancient Jewish Feast of the Pentecost. Their number was once again twelve: Matthias, their new member, had been chosen by lot to replace Judas, who had hung himself out of remorse. During the Pentecost celebration, "a sound came from heaven like a rush of a mighty wind, and it filled all the house where they were sitting." (Acts 2:2) The apostles "were all filled with the Holy Spirit and began to speak in other tongues, as the Spirit gave them utterance." (Acts 2:4) This Descent of the Holy Spirit marks the founding of the church, because the apostles could now speak in all languages and so spread Christ's word throughout the world. Peter, who was to become the first pope, explained the event to the bewildered multitude and then told them, "Repent, and be baptized every one of you in the name of Jesus Christ for the forgiveness of your sins; and you shall receive the gift of the Holy Spirit." (Acts 2:38) The cycle of salvation that began with *The Expulsion of Joachim from the Temple* ends here as mankind awaits the Last Judgment.

In the quatrefoil is the story of *Moses Receiving the Tablets of the Law*, an Old Testament miracle viewed as a precursor to the Pentecost.

39. *The Last Judgment*

This fresco, the largest in the Scrovegni Chapel, covers the entire entrance wall and is the last image visitors see as they leave the chapel. It is a graphic and inescapable reminder of the Second Coming of Christ, which will close the sequence of sacred events commenced by His incarnation in the Annunciation depicted directly across the chapel on the chancel wall. On this day, the dead will be resurrected and, along with the living, judged and consigned either to eternal life or eternal damnation.

The painting of *The Last Judgment* presented Giotto with a number of difficult problems. There was the sheer dimensions of the fresco, which was to be many times the size of the other painted stories. In addition, any depiction of *The Last Judgment* necessitated the inclusion of many disparate elements—the judging Christ, Satan, heaven, hell, the apostles, angels—that were difficult to harmonize, especially for a painter like Giotto, who strove always for a tightly controlled, pared-down narrative. And, in fact, he was unable to find a clear, coherent structure for *The*

Judgment, which seems to surge across the wall like some great iconographic machine whose size and complexity make it difficult to grasp as a whole. Moreover, the rigid groups of angels around the windows and the ranks of the blessed at the right hand of Christ make a jarring contrast to the disorganized, contorted bodies of the damned surrounding the huge Satan in the lower right of the fresco.

Depictions of the contorted gyrations and punishments of the damned in hell are usually of more visual interest to the painter than the placid realm of heaven and the blessed, and Giotto was at his inventive best in the terrified little sinners who are snatched up by Satan. Throughout *The Last Judgment*, the quality of design and the execution of the figures varies substantially, suggesting that Giotto let his assistants do much of this enormous painting.

Detail of hell, *The Last Judgment*

40a., 40b. *Fortitude* and *Inconstancy*

Giotto painted fourteen personifications of the Virtues and Vices in fictive marble niches below the lowest registers of frescoes on the side walls of the Scrovegni Chapel. The Virtues are on the right wall, the Vices on the Left. The right wall is on the side of heaven in *The Last Judgment*, while the left wall is on the side of hell in that fresco. The message of the Virtues and Vices is simple: Virtue leads to heaven and Vice to hell. Each Virtue is paired with a corresponding Vice set directly across the chapel, so that they form seven pairs; all of these small figures are painted in grisaille to look like marble statues.

Before Giotto, the Virtues and Vices could be recognized only by identifying inscriptions or by attributes. But in the Scrovegni Chapel, each figure is expressive of the particular Virtue or Vice it represents. In *Fortitude*, for example, the massive, rooted body fits securely and easily within the niche. The columnar fluting of the robe and the large shield further integrate the figure within its setting. The stable and steady expression of form in *Fortitude* is entirely lacking in *Inconstancy*, whose body and pose are the visual embodiment of that state of mind. Precariously riding a wheel down an incline, her outflung arms and billowing robes in strong opposition to the niche, *Inconstancy* seems about to careen out into the observer's space. The meanings of the Virtues and Vices are, like the meaning of the narratives above them, enhanced and enlarged by comparison.

FORTITVDO